WHITE STAR PUBLISHERS

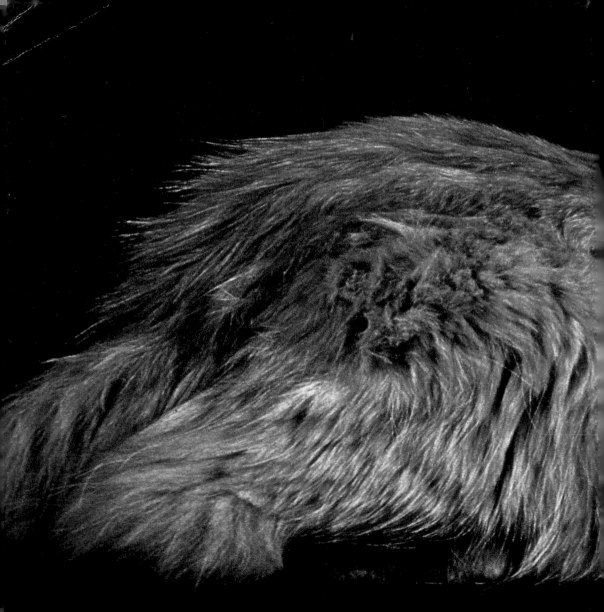

# TEXT BY

CATERINA GROMIS DI TRANA

**project manager
and editorial director**
VALERIA MANFERTO DE FABIANIS

**editorial coordination**
GIADA FRANCIA

**graphic design**
CLARA ZANOTTI

**editorial staff**
ENRICO LAVAGNO
ALBERTO BERTOLAZZI

**translation**
AMY CHRISTINE EZRIN

© 2005 WHITE STAR S.P.A.
VIA CANDIDO SASSONE, 22-24
13100 VERCELLI - ITALY
WWW.WHITESTAR.IT

ISBN 88-544-0076-9

REPRINTS:
1 2 3 4 5 6  09 08 07 06 05

Printed in China
Color separation: Mycrom, Turin

# CONTENTS

## CATS

*1* • Curiosity and tenderness in this month-old cat.

*2-3* • A Cymric adult exemplar.

*4-5* • A Chinchilla family: a mother and her four kittens.

*6-7* • Playful and lazy, a little Ragdoll kitten stretches.

*9* • Kittens playing: an image common to every race and species.

*11* • The intense expression of a Persian cat.

*12-13* • Curiosity: four little European tabbies at a window.

*14-15* • Accompanied by their mother, the kittens go off to explore the outdoors.

# Introduction

THERE ARE THOSE THAT ADORE THEM AND THOSE THAT DETEST THEM, DEPENDING ON PERSONAL POINTS OF VIEW: AFFECTIONATE, DISCREET, AND VELVETY COMPANIONS OR SNEAKY, GOOD-FOR-NOTHING FREELOADERS. THEY HAVE COMPLICATED PERSONALITIES, FULL OF NUANCES WITH LITTLE TRANSPARENCY. TO TRY TO UNDERSTAND THEM, IT MAY BE NECESSARY TO LIVE WITH ONE OF THEM; OTHERWISE, THEY REMAIN IDEAS, DAYDREAMS, OR MISUNDERSTOOD ENIGMAS.

THEY DIFFER ACCORDING TO PERSONALITY, BREED, UPBRINGING, AND EXPERIENCE. MY CHILDHOOD CAT WAS A FEMALE. HER NAME WAS BAFFA AND SHE WAS BLACK AND CRANKY, ADORABLE IN MY EYES. LITTLE INCLINED TO RUB

● The funny behavior of a tabby kitten.

# Introduction

UP AGAINST YOU OR TO ACT SUPER SWEET, SHE WAS PROUD AND DIGNIFIED. SHE PURRED IN MODERATION, WITHOUT EXCESS, IF YOU SOFTLY SCRATCHED UNDER HER CHIN WHILE SHE DOZED CURLED UP. WHEN SHE WAS NOT IN THE MOOD, SHE GOT UP AND WENT OFF, BUT THEN CAME BACK TO OFFER ME HER PREY: POOR, HALF-DEAD MICE. IN THIS WAY, CATS MAKE THEIR GREATEST GESTURE OF HONOR TO THEIR OWNER, TREATING THEM ALMOST LIKE A KITTEN TO BE CARED FOR. ONE DAY, SHE ESCAPED TO THE COURTYARD OF OUR APARTMENT BUILDING AND DISAPPEARED. TO CONSOLE ME, I WAS GIVEN A SIAMESE CAT WITH LIGHT-BLUE EYES, AFFECTIONATE AND GORGEOUS, ALMOST MORE LIKE A DOG THAN A CAT, NAMED BAFFO IN

# Introduction

MEMORY. HE LASTED ONLY A FEW MONTHS; HE WAS STOLEN WHILE STILL A BABY. THEN, ONE FINE DAY, A BLACK CAT CROSSED THE COURTYARD AND ENTERED OUR HOUSE CONFIDENTLY, AS IF SHE KNEW WHERE TO GO. WHO KNOWS IF IT WAS BAFFA HERSELF, MISSING BY THEN FOR A YEAR? SHE MADE HERSELF RIGHT AT HOME, THOUGH CATS ARE KNOWN TO CHOOSE THEIR DWELLING QUICKLY IF SOME-ONE WELCOMES THEM, AND I WAS WAITING FOR HER. IT IS NOT TRUE THAT CATS LOVE THEIR HOUSE BUT DO NOT GIVE AFFECTION TO THEIR OWNER. RATHER, THEY DO NOT KNOW THE MEANING OF THE WORD "OWNER." THE NEW BAFFA FELT AS IF SHE WERE THE MASTER OF THE HOUSE, THE EQUAL OF ITS OTHER INHABITANTS, AND LIVED MANY YEARS.

## Introduction

A BOOK ON CATS DESCRIBES THEM THROUGH FASCINAT-
ING IMAGES, LIKE PERSONALITY REVEALING ICONS. LEAFING
THROUGH THEM IS LIKE ENTERING A DÉJÀ-VU WORLD:
EVEN THOSE WHO HAVE NEVER HAD A CAT AT HOME KNOW
THEIR MOVEMENTS AND POSTURE, BECAUSE CATS ARE
EVERYWHERE AND EVERYONE HAS HAD AN OPPORTUNITY
TO MEET ONE, AND EVEN IF THEY LOOK WITHOUT OBSERV-
ING, SOMETHING REMAINS. THIS BOOK CAN BE A WISH FOR
THE FUTURE, TO REMEMBER A LOVED FELINE, TO DISCOV-
ER ONE, OR EVEN TO SIMPLY MEET A CAT IN THE STREET
AND STOP, ENCHANTED, TO WATCH IT.

# NOBLE
# PEDIGREES

A long-haired Persian shows its round green eyes.

## INTRODUCTION Noble Pedigrees

Cats will not be commanded and can choose their own owner. Thus, man has selected cats of pedigree over common cats. The idea is recent: cats were only cats until the nineteenth century, when the first feline exhibition was held at the Crystal Palace in London. At the time, the competition was reserved to only two competitors, the Persian and the stiff-haired British cat. Later, associations, feline federations, and rules were established, and today the recognized breeds number more than 100. In the fascinating search for a harmonious breed, whether stocky or slender, eastern or common, the feline associations serve to reward commendable initiatives

## **INTRODUCTION** Noble Pedigrees

AND KEEP EXCESSIVE EFFORTS IN CHECK. ON ONE HAND, THERE IS THE EXAMPLE OF THE BENGALI CAT, A CROSS BETWEEN A SMALL WILD CAT WIDESPREAD IN SOUTHEAST ASIA AND A SHORT-HAIR DOMESTIC CAT, CREATED THANKS TO RESEARCH ON FELINE LEUKEMIA. ON THE OTHER HAND, THERE IS THE CASE OF THE SPHINX CAT, HAIRLESS, AFFECTIONATE BY NATURE, AND SOFT LIKE SUEDE, BUT WHICH CANNOT SURVIVE OUTSIDE OF WELL-HEATED HOUSES. THE MUTATION THAT MAKES IT INTER-ESTING IS TO THE DETRIMENT OF ITS AND ITS SUCCES-SORS' HEALTH, HENCE THE BREED IS NOT OFFICIALLY RECOGNIZED. EVERYONE HAS THEIR FAVORITE BREED. THERE ARE THOSE WHO LOVE TO CARE FOR THE COATS OF SOPHISTICATED PERSIANS. OTHERS ARE ENCHANTED

# Noble Pedigrees

Introduction

BY THE DOUBLY THICK FUR OF THE NORWEGIAN FOREST CAT, THE ELF CAT OF SCANDINAVIAN FABLES, PLAYFUL AND SWEET, WHICH ADORES PEOPLE. SOME CHOOSE THE IMPERTINENCE OF SIAMESE CATS, OUT-GOING AND NOISY. FULL-BRED CATS ARE ARISTOCRATIC IN BEARING AND BEHAVIOR, BUT THEIR GENEALOGICAL TREE IS NOT SO ANCIENT, NO MORE THAN A CENTURY OLD. IT CAN BE NOTED IN SOMETHING, ITS FELINE NATURE, NOT YET TRAINED BY HISTORY TO THE DISCIPLINE THAT ONLY THE OLDEST FAMILIES HAVE. IF LET FREE TO DO AS IT WANTS, IT WILL COUPLE WITH WHOM IT WANTS, AND WITHIN A GENERATION, OR AT MOST TWO, WILL GO BACK TO BEING A COMMON CAT. CATS ARE ALWAYS CATS.

• This Abyssinian's pose is very distinguished.

# Oriental

34 • Of medium size, the Oriental Shorthair is slim and elegant.

35 • The nose is a perfect triangle, under big ears.

36 ● The striped coat is highly appreciated by lovers of this breed.

37 ● Long and slender limbs characterize the Oriental's appearance.

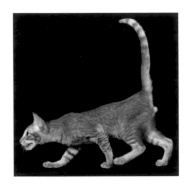

● According to experts, the personality
of Orientals resembles that of Siamese,
from which they originated. They are very
friendly and affectionate cats, but also
always ready to play.

● Breeders have been very careful in creating the coat. These two exemplars belong to the spotted variety: the color seems spread about the hair with a paintbrush.

Almond-shaped eyes give exemplars of this breed an intense and enigmatic gaze, slightly softened by the green or blue color of the iris.

# Sacred Cat of Burma

44 ● The coat of the Birman, also known as the Sacred Cat of Burma,
is generally of one kind, called "Himalayan" or "Colorpoint."

45 ● The round blue eyes and soft fur make this cat a beloved
and pleasant roommate for an apartment.

46-47 ● Shy and docile, the Birman likes peace and quiet.

*48 and 49* ● White paws are characteristic of this breed: legend has it that they have been this color since an exemplar came into contact with a dying monk before he released his last breath.

*50-51* ● Birman cats were introduced to the West at the beginning of the twentieth century. The first exemplars came to France, where the breed was further refined by skillful breeding.

# Somali

52 ● The Somali cat is very popular with cat lovers, who appreciate its nice blend
of wild traits with an affectionate nature.

53 ● Lively eyes and a muscular body, these Somali cats – two kittens and their mother – boast
gorgeous, thick, reddish-colored fur, called "usual."

# Chartreux

54 ● The light draws rather robust features on the soft fur of this Chartreux cat.

55 ● A round head and chubby cheeks, the Chartreux inspires both tenderness and respect.

*56-57* ● Cats of this breed are very popular in France, the place where it seems they were bred for the first time.

*58-59* ● Little Chartreux kittens have light stripes, which disappear with age.

*60-61* ● A mother with her son, captured at strange moment. Their characteristic bluish-gray fur takes on slivery hues around the nose.

# Ragdoll

62 • In the Ragdoll's veins runs the blood of at least three other breeds (Burmese, Persian, and Birman) as well as that of the common cat.

63 • The result of the breeding is a docile and affectionate cat, with a robust but elegant build.

Ragdoll kittens are dependent on their mothers for longer than those of other races. This is probably because of their slower growth; it takes three years for the Ragdoll to fully develop.

A sort of gray paint-stroke marks this kitten's face, already lively with its intense blue eyes.

Lazy and sleepy, this kitten belongs to the bicolor variety.

Ragdolls get their name from a side of their personality. Mild and quiet, they willingly let themselves be cuddled, sitting extremely relaxed in their owner's arms, just like a rag doll.

# American Curl

- The typical ears
of the American Curl
characterize the head.
They fold back, are set
far apart, and are
covered by tufts of hair.

74 ● At birth, Curls have straight ears. They only begin to fold after a few weeks.

75 ● The gene that causes the ear mutation is dominant, but recessive in cross-breeds. This can result in Curls with less curled or even straight ears.

The coat, above all in the type with medium-length hair, is soft, silky, and can be found in a wide variety of colors.

# Ocicat

78 ● The name Ocicat comes from the ocelot, a wild feline with a gorgeous spotted coat.

79 ● With an elongated head, triangular ears, and almond-shaped eyes, the Ocicat has a rather strange appearance and a very intelligent expression.

80 ● Even though they are rather robust, cats of this breed have the grace typical of Asian cats.

81 ● Their coat, wonderfully spotted, can feature a variety of colorations.

# Exotic

- The peaceful look of this Exotic cat may be misleading: it is a very robust cat and a skillful hunter, besides curious and intelligent.

84 ● The expression of this striped Exotic cat leaves no doubt: it is having a moment of pleasant relaxation.

85 ● According to breeders, the striped variety with a reddish coat must have orange irises.

The standard look of the Exotic is more or less that of the long-haired Persian, of which it is a variation.

● Exotics have a very
balanced temperament
and love human
company.

# Persian

- Persians are probably the most famous cat breed in the world. Normally, they have long and fine hair, which requires continuous care.

Persian kittens
feature the typical
characteristics of adults:
round eyes,
chubby cheeks,
and a short
and wide nose.

94 ● Cats of this breed are robust and muscular and have an aristocratic bearing.

95 ● The peaceful expression of this exemplar reveals the true nature of the Persian breed.

96 • The symmetry of the coat, apparent on the face of this kitty, is one of the obligatory characteristics of the multicolor variety.

97 • Large orange eyes open wide with curiosity, giving this Persian a very lively look.

● Their long, highly prized fur gives Persians an almost regal air. These two cats seem aware and proud of it.

● Persians probably descend from the Angora cat, brought to Europe in the days of the earliest voyages to the East. By crossbreeding the Angora with cats of various types during the 1800s, the breed as we know it today was created.

The coat reaches its maximum fullness in winter. As warmer weather approaches, the fur becomes thinner and more attractive.

Originally, Persians were white, like their progenitors from Angora. After various crossings, other colors took hold, but white continues to be the most highly prized.

- Mistakenly considered lazy, Persians
are actually composed,
even-tempered, and not usually
quarrelsome.

*108 and 109* ● The kittens of this breed are true balls of down.

*110-111* ● Perhaps because of their haughty bearing, Persians were long the favorite cats of the European aristocracy.

*112-113* ● The flattened face is actually the result of recent breeding.

# Chinchilla

114 • Two Chinchilla kittens huddle together, perhaps scared by the photographers' lens. All the curiosity of kittens can be seen in their eyes.

115 • The Chinchilla is a particularly prized variety of the Persian. Among the most obvious characteristics, it has a less flattened nose and a slightly protruding forehead.

# Javanese

116 ● The Javanese cat is a sub-breed of the medium-length-haired Oriental.
It is an excellent companion, affection, and lively.

117 ● The gaze of this cat betrays its curiosity and intelligence, characteristics noticed
in all exemplars of its breed.

# Balinese

118 ● Balinese cats look much like Siamese, despite having longer and thicker coats.

119 ● The intense gaze of this Balinese reveals the lively and energetic
nature of this cat.

A lovely litter of kittens poses for the camera, ears tense and eyes wide open.

# British Shorthair

- In two different poses,
these British Shorthair
exemplars summarize
the characteristics
of the breed: curiosity,
expressiveness,
and vigor.

The British is probably the most widespread short-haired cat in Europe. Adaptable and docile, it was bred in Great Britain at the beginning of the twentieth century.

● The British Shorthair was bred in a large variety of colors and coats. The mostly white multicolor version is called Harlequin or Van.

## Devon Rex

In Devon Rex litters, the main characteristic of the breed stands out for physiological reasons. long neck and wide ears, with big intense and expressive eyes.

# Cornish Rex

130 ● A Cornish Rex dashes off with a leap, exploiting its innate agility.

131 ● The typical curly fur of the Cornish features notable advantages: not subject to shedding, this cat is a ideal companion for allergy sufferers.

# Selkirk Rex

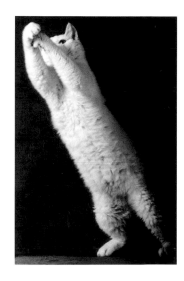

● Having selected its prey (left),
the Selkirk Rex launches its attack
(right). Even if its robust build makes
it look like a little bear, the Selkirk
is very agile and fast.

# Norwegian Forest Cat

*134 and 135* ● The Norwegian, like all long-haired cats, must trace its origins back to
a geographical area between southern Russia and Ancient Persia.

*136-137* ● The quality of the fur, thick and soft, is a characteristic of this breed.

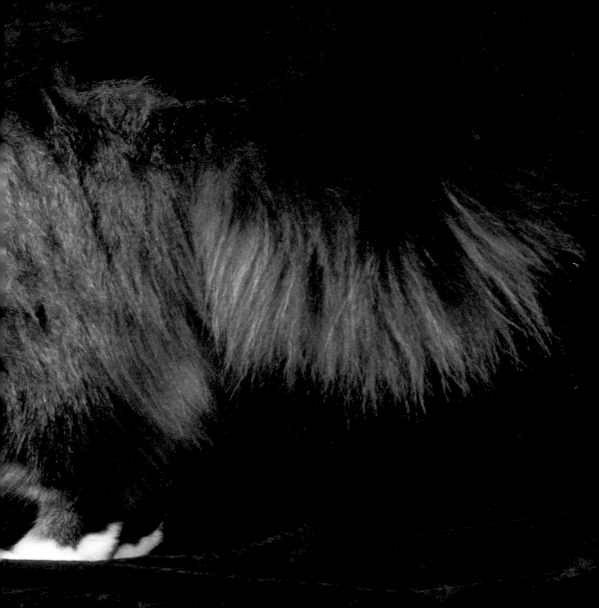

138 ● Intrigued, this Norwegian stands up on two paws, demonstrating an unsuspected agility.

139 ● The eyes of this exemplar, still round, prove its young age. As it grows up, they will tend to take on an almond shape.

140 ● Even when it sheds, during the warm season, the big soft tail retains its full thickness.

141 ● With a peaceful nature, the Norwegian knows how to be lively and active. It loves liberty, although it does not disdain the warmth of apartments.

Exemplars of this breed are excellent climbers and love to hunt.

# Angora

144 • The soft medium-length fur of Angora cats is legendary.

145 • The result of several crossings, this cat of Asian origin loves human company and needs constant care and affection.

Angoras are strong, willful, and very lively and love to play.

Cousins of the short-haired Oriental cats, Angoras have a thick and shiny coat even when young.

# Ceylon

- Docile and meek, the Ceylon cat features a short coat of the characteristic Alu Pata color, renamed Manilla in the West, from the island of Sri Lanka.

*152-153* ● Though the Ceylon has controversial origins, it seems proven to be a natural breed, meaning its origin is not the result of manipulation or breeding.

*153* ● The color Manilla is distinguished by a soft apricot hue with golden shades, onto which is added a sort of black dotting.

*154-155* ● In nature, it is possible to find exemplars featuring coats of different colors. Purists accept beige, red, and black.

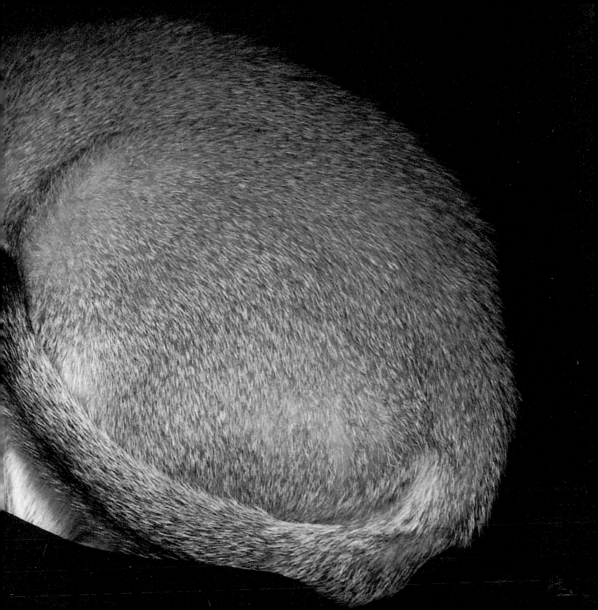

# Burmese

● The Burmese has mysterious origins,
probably earlier than 1700.
Similar to Siamese, it was imported
to the West by an American doctor
in the early 1930s.

● Two distinct genealogies exist for Burmese cats: the American one prefers cats of a robust build (left), whereas the British one favors a more slender Eastern standard. More than physical characteristics, the coloration of its coat determined the success of the breed.

Kittens of this breed are playful and affectionate. Not at all quarrelsome, they love to be pet and keep this characteristic throughout life.

# Manx

● The Manx breed developed
on the Isle of Man a few
centuries ago. They are mainly
characterized by a stubby or
even non-existent tail.

# Scottish Fold

164 ● The sweet gaze of this Scottish Fold suggests a sociable and affectionate nature.

165 ● The Scottish Fold is known by enthusiasts throughout the world for its funny bent ears, which make it look like an owl.

166-167 ● Cats of this breed, gorgeous with their healthy glow, conceal a genetic fragility: to avoid the risk of deformities, they must not interbreed.

# Siberian

168 ● Very similar to the Norwegian, the Siberian is widespread in Eastern Europe and Russia.

169 ● Among the characteristics of this breed stand out the long tufts sticking up from the ears and the thick and shiny coat.

## Maine Coon

● The Maine Coon
may be the most
popular feline in the
United States.
Large and very robust,
exemplars of this
breed are the biggest
domestic cats
existent.

*172 and 172-173* ● The name Maine comes from the American state in which the breed was first documented. Coon, on the other hand, is an abbreviation of the word "raccoon."

*174-175* ● The physical characteristics of this breed have fed various legends: one of these recounts that the Maine Coon was a cross between a cat and a raccoon.

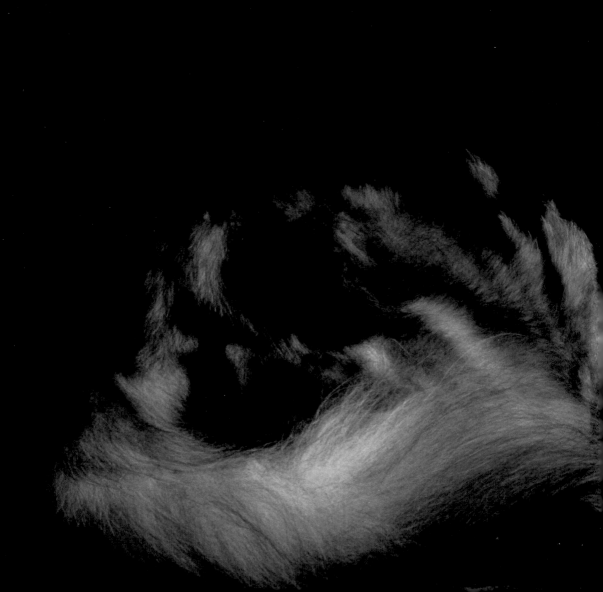

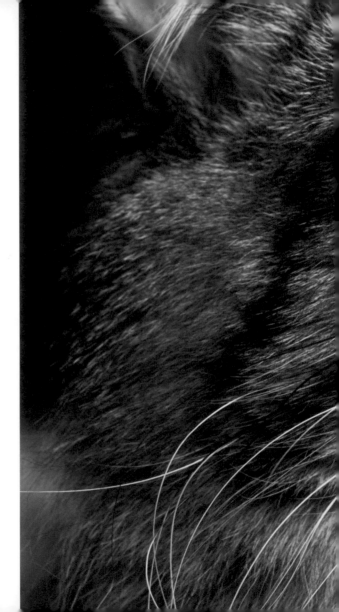

The big oval eyes, slightly angled, and the tufts of fur that stick up from the ears recall the close relation between this breed and the long-haired breeds from Northeastern Europe.

# Sphinx

178 ● Sinuous and elegant, the Sphinx has a mysterious and surprising look.

179 ● The big elongated eyes, placed on a perfectly triangular head, topped by disproportionately large hearing auricles, give this cat an enigmatic Eastern-like charm.

180 ● Exemplars of this breed are born and die completely bald, boasting ancient ancestors among the hairless cats of the Aztecs.

181 ● Although their appearance raises some reverential fear, cats of this breed are nice and peaceful.

Considered hairless, Sphinx cats are actually covered by a thin and dense fur, which protects them from sunburn. The apparent lack of fur emphasizes the morphological characteristics of this breed: hind legs longer than the front ones, a long and slender tail, and a triangular head.

Behind the surprised expression of these exemplars, there is intelligence and innate curiosity.

186 ● The Sphinx have big paws with highly developed pads,
accentuating their uniqueness.

187 ● All the atypical expressiveness of the Sphinx is concentrated
in this defensive pose.

## Singapura

A thin build and a
coat with unusual
blurred color coat on
an ivory base
characterizes cats of
the Singapore breed.

All the curiosity and tenderness of which a feline is capable is found in the expression of this cat.

# Abyssinian

192 ● Even though there is no historical proof, many believe that the Abyssinian was a breed beloved in Egypt in the days of the pharaohs.

193 ● Thin and of obvious Eastern origin, this Abyssinian exemplar exudes liveliness and curiosity.

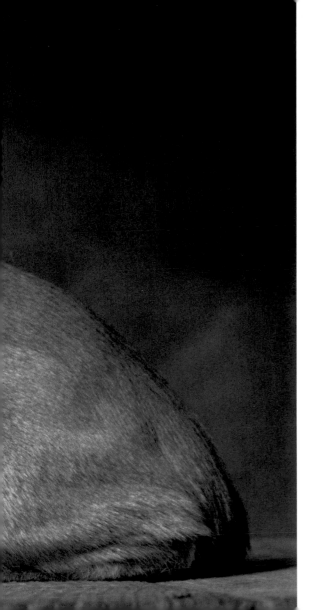

194-195 ● Abyssinians have thin limbs and, in general, a rather tiny build.

195 ● The question-mark-shaped tail communicates the circumspect intentions of this exemplar.

*196 and 197* • Lively and playful like all kittens, little Abyssinians are very intelligent
and learn with great speed.

*198-199* • From when they are babies, cats of this breed feature the characteristic
color on their fur. The color of these two kittens, called "usual,"
is also the most widespread.

Abyssinians with "silver" fur are very common but also a topic of disagreement among feline associations. The silvery colorations on the downy fur are, however, highly prized by lovers of these cats.

Felines with an outstanding personality, Abyssinians know how to defend themselves well against enemies. However, they are not nasty and can weave "friendly" relationships even with dogs.

# Bengali

*204 and 205* ● The Bengali most resemble the wild felines of the jungle. The fur recalls that there was, at the origin of this breed, a cross between domestic cats and the wild Leopard cat.

*206-207* ● A leap worthy of a big feline: agility and strength are characteristics of the Bengali.

*208-209* ● Bengali cats can have spotted coats or, as in this case, striped, but their tails always end with a black point.

# Siamese

● Even to the eyes of amateurs, the thin
build and shaded coat represent
distinctive traits of the Siamese, one of
the most famous and prized breeds in
the world.

212 ● Of a strong and willful temperament, the Siamese is capable of great shows of affection towards its owner.

213 ● The short and silky fur of cats of this breed is shaded in an unmistakable manner on the feet and nose.

The flexibility and agility of the Siamese are evident in this brief sequence.

# European

216 ● A family of short-hair Europeans looks into the camera. The little ones already show the characteristic striped markings on their fur.

217 ● The European is intelligent and playful but also possesses a special and well-developed hunting instinct.

# Bobtail Japanese

218 ● The Bobtail Japanese is also known as the Japanese Short Tail,
in reference to its most apparent peculiarity.

219 ● Two kittens and their mother look out the window; the white marks on their head
look like parts in their "hair" and emphasize their lovely expressiveness.

220-221 ● In this relaxed and almost "human" pose, the Bobtail Japanese radiates charming intelligence.

222-223 ● Crouched, perhaps for a projected ambush, this exemplar features gorgeous green almond-shaped eyes and intense black and red marks, which the Japanese call "mi-ke."

# Little Clowns
## Introduction

PREVAIL. IT IS TRAINING. A FUTURE PREDATOR MUST KNOW HOW TO ATTACK AND FLEE, IN ADDITION TO CATCHING AND CLUTCHING. INSTINCT DOES NOT LACK, BUT WITHOUT THIS INDOCTRINATION PROCESS DURING THE FIRST WEEKS OF LIFE, A CAT WILL NEVER BECOME A GOOD HUNTER. HUNTING IS AN ART THAT IS PASSED DOWN; IT IS NOT THE LAST CHANCE FOR STARVING CATS, BUT RATHER A GAME AND PROFESSION. THE IMAGE OF KITTENS GENERATES POSITIVE FEELINGS AND BRINGS OUT PATIENCE IN THE MOTHER. THAT STUFFED-ANIMAL APPEARANCE IS NOT A COINCIDENCE: IT HELPS THEM TO GROW UP HAPPY AND CODDLED WHILE PLAYING. THE FELINE NATURE TEACHES HOW TO LEARN WHILE HAVING FUN.

- Lounging on the lawn, warmed by the heat of the sun, a little European lets himself go with a yawn.

It is not more than a month old, and yet this bicolored kitten is already as active and cautious as an adult.

With limited movement because of its still immature physical structure, this little cat does not forgo a beneficial gallop across the grass.

234 ● Born to parents of different races, bearers of genes of all kinds, kittens of the same litter can be very different from each other.

235 ● These three Maine Coon, on the other hand, are very similar, both in coat and in behavior.

● The innate curiosity of kittens leads them to leap over any obstacle to see, fearless, what hides behind. The expression on this Maine Coon confirms this fact.

*238-239* ● A fish in a bowl is the incarnation of what the kitten wants but cannot have, at least until it concocts some strategy to reach its coveted prey.

*240-241* ● A small Maine Coon leans against a flower-lined fence, as if it wanted to pose for the photographer.

A few bicolored kittens not more than three weeks old venture onto a lawn, still uncertain, as seen in the expressions on their faces, about their movements.

● One month old, this little European has already taken on the marked features of its breed and acquired a certain confidence in its movements.

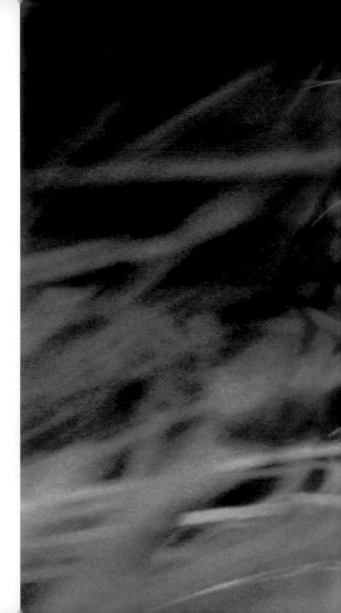

A lovely Persian kitten crouched in the grass seems to wait for its prey to make a false move.

● Exploration of the outdoors happens in the first weeks, even if kittens rarely dare to stray from their mother. Their siblings' company can, however, spur and encourage even the most fearful.

250 ● The head of a Maine Coon sticks
out of the tall grass, like a submarine
periscope.

250-251 ● In the first month,
the personality of every cat is formed.
During this time, its future will be decided.

These kittens seem to want to blend into the bark of a tree, apparently attracted by a potential "victim."

Wrestling and nasty skirmishes are the
favorite games of young cats, through
which they acquire an understanding
of their own bodies.

Tiny acrobats, kittens take unexpected leaps to reach any moving object, in this case a rope

*258* • Suspended, clinging with all its strength to a rope, this kitten is
the incarnation of agility.

*259* • With its fur ruffled by the wind, a little Maine Coon plays with the hanging laundry.

• A straw hat is a hiding place and a game, ideal for a young European in good health.

The ability to climb, dependent upon
the innate gifts of agility and strength,
comes out within the early weeks
of a kitten's life.

The preparatory phases of an ambush and the instant immediately before: the victim has no choice but to be subjected to attack...

*266* ● Four Maine Coon have got into a tub, from which they watch the world, like a specially reserved observatory.

*266-267* ● After having found warm shelter, this kitten slips into a lazy stupor, a prelude to sleep.

Even a ladder or a leafy branch can become additional athletic equipment for these phenomenal acrobats.

An insect or an aromatic flower is an extraordinary toy for any kitten.

These unusual expressions are part of a much vaster repertory, including joy, fear, anger, tenderness...

With a stare fixed upon its prey, muscles immobile, this kitten is a perfect predator in miniature.

● The meow of each kitten is unmistakable to its mother, able to recognize it from a distance and among a thousand other calls.

● Hunting insects and butterflies is one of the favorite hobbies of kittens during summer. The two exemplars portrayed do not mind inventing the most outrageous solutions to reach their prey.

*280* ● Putting their nose into bags and boxes is part of the collection of instincts of any good kitten.

*280-281* ● Perhaps attracted more by the container than the edibility of its contents, this European kitten seems undecided about what to do.

*282 and 283* ● Brothers in eternal battle, these two kittens compete for the spot on the wall to the sound of "slaps."

*284-285* ● The low head and short step suggests that this kitten is tracking some interesting prey.

286 ● Sometimes playful, sometimes lazy and sluggish, kittens reflect the behavior of adult cats in every way.

287 ● Captured by a photographer at a quiet moment, these three little Europeans seem intent on resting, but the hooked tail of one of them raises suspicion that they might start to play again.

Agile like panthers, acrobatic like leopards, kittens are able to overcome obstacles in their surroundings within their first months.

290 ● Just a few days old, this kitten's gaze is still veiled and bewildered. In two weeks, it will gain self-confidence and assuredness.

291 ● The little cats show characteristics common to all mammal babies: a big head and eyes, short and chubby legs, and a thin but insistent voice.

A bird or an insect can hold the attention of kittens, out to discover the world, for hours.

• Wrestling is for play, but also a means to learn the difficult but crucial art of self-defense.

Every nook or cranny
is worth exploring,
every hole an ideal den.

298 ● A page of a newspaper can be a roof and an enclosure, making the outdoors
a little less vast and dangerous.

299 ● Sheltered by an improvised paper hut, this little Maine Coon seems to observe
the world with greater certainty.

The black and the yellow: black, the solid coat of this gorgeous kitten, yellow, the wool that cushions the basket, and yellow, the expressive eyes of this miniature panther.

*302-303* ● Fur, particularly if it is long and abundant like with this seven-week-old Persian cat, must be brushed regularly: parasites and even grave illnesses always lie in wait.

*304-305* ● The little sleepy eyes betray an age somewhere between two and three weeks for these kittens, hidden timidly in a basket.

*From 306 to 309* ● The ambush of, the approach towards, and the attack upon a victim are the three critical phases of hunting, techniques that kittens learn in the first months of life by playing and imitating their parents.

*310* ● Ready to leap, this kitten launches its weight off its hind legs like a spring.

*311* ● Bothered by a parasite or some skin irritation, a Maine Coon kitten gives itself
a good scratch.

312 • Typically feline, this defensive behavior is instinctive to cats and is present in kittens from birth.

313 • Stretching after a good sleep is also healthy for the young and nimble muscles of little cats.

● Capable of unpredictable twists and bends, felines have an extraordinary tendency towards acrobatics and contortions.

*316 and 317* ● Attempting to grab flying prey and hiss at potential threats are two typically feline behaviors, which inspire tenderness and sweetness.

*318-319* ● Four kittens of the same litter: each one clearly bears a part of its parents' genetic heritage on its coat.

The concentration of which a kitten is capable is legendary: nothing exists besides its prey, not even the laws of physics...

Portrayed in a position of surprise and during a heaven-sent scratch, this little Maine Coon seems to possess the innate grace of which only kittens can boast.

● Despite their massive and robust build, emphasized by their thick fur, Persians are very agile. This kitten, busy with two different games, demonstrates this fact.

A colorful toy, simulating a mouse, is about to end up between the claws of this fearsome hunter, capable of incredible acrobatic feats.

- A ball of colored wool can make a kitten as happy as a clam, playing with it until it is completely unraveled.

● Irritated by the unpredictable opposition of the ball of wool, this kitten prepares to take on the "enemy" with its fearsome claws.

*332* ● Elegant and composed, this kitten looks like the consummate model, born to be portrayed by photographers.

*333* ● Attracted by some hanging object, this little Maine Coon holds all the vitality and curiosity innate in kittens in its eyes.

# FAMILY LIFE

● A tender embrace between two Burmese cats. The little one, about one month old,
is still completely dependent on motherly care.

## INTRODUCTION Family Life

Days spent in perfect harmony: from birth, kittens get exclusive possession of a nipple, which will always be the same one for each sibling so that they have nothing to fight over. It is a blessed life, revolving only around maintaining their happiness, while their mother watches lovingly over her brood. As adults, something stays in their memory of those early, carefree days, that regular pace, slow and deliberate, rhythmic, which domestic cats take, accompanied by a sonorous purr and abundant saliva, in the lap of their so-called owner. They seem to be walking, but they are actually repeating the movements they made as newborns, when they pressed

## INTRODUCTION Family Life

AGAINST THE WARM BELLY OF THEIR MOTHER TO STIMU-
LATE THE FLOW OF MILK TO THE TEAT. THEIR MOUTH WA-
TERS AND THEY ARE NOISILY HAPPY. THEIR OWNER MUST
KNOW HOW TO BE A SUBSTITUTE MOTHER AND A REASON
FOR THEIR FAVORITE SON TO RETURN TO HIS INFANCY.

TO SPITE A LITTER OF SUCKLING KITTENS, JUST WASH THE
BELLY OF THEIR MOTHER. THE LITTLE ONES RECOGNIZE
THEIR PERSONAL NIPPLE BY SMELL, BUT IF THIS DISAP-
PEARS, THEY SEARCH AROUND DISORIENTED. ABOUT
TWENTY OR SO DAYS AFTER GIVING BIRTH, IT SHOULD BE
TIME FOR THE MOTHER CAT TO DO WHAT INSTINCT COM-
MANDS HER TO DO: GRAB HER KITTENS BY THE SCRUFF
AND MOVE THEM, ONE BY ONE, TO A NEW RESTING PLACE.
THE KITTENS, JUGGLED LIKE MARIONETTES, REMAIN STIFF

# Family Life
## Introduction

IN A CARRYING POSITION, SILENT AND OBEDIENT. THE FEMALE CAT IS NOT HOSTILE TOWARDS THE BIRTH PLACE, BUT THE TIME HAS COME IN LIFE AND IN THE WILD WHEN THE KITTENS MUST LEARN TO BITE AND CHEW THE PREY THAT THEIR MOTHER WILL CATCH FOR THEM. HUNTING LESSONS MUST BE HELD ON-SITE, AND THE INITIAL SAFE AND PROTECTED SHELTER, PERFECT FOR HELPLESS ONES, IS NO LONGER SUITABLE. EVERYTHING PROCEEDS IN STAGES AT THE BEGINNING, WHEN ONLY THE MOTHER AND SIBLINGS EXIST IN A KITTEN'S WORLD: BRAWLS FOR FUN, AMBUSHES FROM THE SHADOWS, PLAY WITH A CAPTURED MOUSE TO TEACH THE OFFSPRING. TIME IS SHORT FOR DRAFTING THE BASICS OF ENTIRE EXISTENCES.

- Hidden under the paws of its mother, this little Scottish Fold seems to want to withdraw from the camera lens.

*340* • This loving exchange of affection between Bengali mother and son falls halfway between hygienic care and demonstrations of affection.

*341* • Carrying a rowdy little one is part of this British Shorthair mother's duties.

● As in other species,
in cats reciprocal
attention serves to
reinforce family ties.

● A kitten a few weeks old jokes with its mother; it is an important moment, seeing how early contact with the outside world occurs through play.

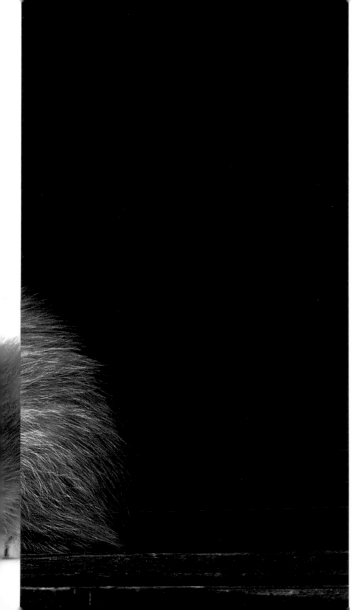

● In all breeds, the
relationship founded
within the first days
between mother
and offspring is
fundamental. Cuddling
and material care also
serve to give
confidence to the
kittens for the difficult
tasks that await them.

With infinite patience, a mother submits to attack by her three kittens.

356 ● Cats normally live between ten and sixteen years. Only a small part of this cycle is spent in close contact with their mother.

357 ● A British Shorthair kitten submits willingly to its mother's care.

358-359 • One of the lessons to be learned quickly: keep away from an unfriendly adult.

360-361 • Playing and imitation of adults constitute the basis for the proper development of kittens: this is the case for this little British Shorthair, busy trying to trap its mother's tail.

# FRIEND or FOE

# FOE

The head of an adult Boxer makes not only for a good observation point but also a safe one.

## INTRODUCTION Friend or Foe

MOTHER NATURE HAS CLASSIFIED FELINES IN THE PREDATOR CATEGORY, OFFERING THEM ONLY TWO CHOICES: ATTACK OR FLEE. CATS HAVE A BRAIN SPECIALIZED IN EVERYTHING RELATIVE TO MOVEMENT: SPRINTING, BALANCE, SPEED, AND DEXTERITY. THEY KNOW HOW TO SURVIVE BY HUNTING AND ARE READY TO ESCAPE.

IN DOMESTIC CATS, THOUSANDS OF YEARS OF CONTACT WITH MAN HAVE CREATED UNUSUAL SITUATIONS, UNEXPECTED ENCOUNTERS, CONSEQUENTIAL ADAPTATIONS, AND NEW BALANCES. IT IS HARD TO ESTABLISH FIXED BEHAVIORAL STANDARDS. SOMETIMES A CAT HAPPENS TO LIVE ON A FARM. FOR IT, THIS PLACE FEATURES THE GREATEST NUMBER OF TRAPS AND TEMPTATION: VICTIM OR ASSASSIN, ITS SENSES ARE ALWAYS ON GUARD. TAUGHT BY

## INTRODUCTION Friend or Foe

MAN, IT CAN MAKE FRIENDS WITH GOATS OR CHICKENS AND CONTROL ITS IMPULSE TO RIP APART THE CHICKS OR RUN AWAY FROM THE DOG OF THE HOUSE. HOWEVER, IT IS BEST TO NOT TRUST THEM TOO MUCH: THOUGH THEY CAN SPEND HOURS SITTING BY A TANK OF GOLDFISH OR A CANARY'S CAGE, IMMOBILE AS IF HYPNOTIZED, THEIR IN-DIFFERENCE IS NOT GUARANTEED. IF DOGS AND CATS GROW UP TOGETHER, AS ADULTS THEY MAY BE ALMOST FRIENDS. IF, ON THE OTHER HAND, THEY ARE STRANGERS WHEN THEY MEET, IT COULD ALL COME DOWN TO A FEW THREATENING GLARES WITH BARED TEETH FROM ONE AND AN INTIMIDATING HUNCHBACK WITH HISSING FROM THE OTHER. OTHERWISE, A REAL CHASE COULD BREAK OUT, WITH A SURPRISE ENDING. IT LOOKS LIKE A RITUAL:

# Friend or Foe

THE DOG CHASES THE CAT, THE CAT IS AFRAID AND ESCAPES TO THE NEAREST TREE. THE DOG JUMPS UP AND DOWN FURIOUSLY BELOW, CAUSING A COMMOTION AS HE TRIES LIKE MAD TO REACH HIS ENEMY, UNTIL HE GIVES UP AND GOES AWAY. AT THAT POINT, THE CAT ALSO SNEAKS OFF. IF, AT A CERTAIN POINT IN THE STORY, THE CAT INTERRUPTS HIS DASH AND STOPS SHORT, THE DOG WILL ALSO FREEZE. EVEN THOUGH HE MAY BE THE BULLY, HE IS ALSO A BIT AFRAID. THEY RARELY COME TO TRUE BLOWS, AS IF THE HUNT AND CHASE WERE A HARMLESS DESIRE, BASED ON ONE PRETEXT: IT IS ALMOST A FORM OF FUN FOR BOTH DOGS AND CATS, DEAR ENEMIES.

- A healthy appetite and a lot of curiosity push a kitten towards an element that it does not love: water.

With friendly skirmishes, useful for building a relationship of mutual tolerance,
a blue tabby kitten plays with a Cavalier-Spitz mix puppy,
as if it were a patient victim.

● Both eight months old, the blue tabby and the mixed breed are pushed by nature itself to not be competitive and to attack only for fun.

Impassive despite the attention it gets, a red cat "does its nails" while examined by the nose of a collie.

*374 and 375* ● Almost affectionate stances for these enemies par excellence.

*376-377* ● Just a colorful object can reconcile the different demeanors of this kitten and puppy, a silver tabby and a border collie.

● Remarkably patient, the silver tabby actually lets himself be "combed" by the border collie, who then becomes the object of its attention: affinity or opportunism?

Between cat and dog,
bonds can be formed
based not only on play:
there seems to be
a certain harmony
even in napping.

Dogs and cats are actually so different in their instincts and habits to have peaceful interaction between them is remarkable. A bit of mutual surprise, therefore, is completely natural.

*From 384 to 389* •
Relative proportions do
not carry much weight
in pacifying dog-cat
relations.

*390 and 391* ● The dachshund seems astounded to see the tabby cat that has appeared nearby. The feline, on its part, does not refuse to accept a contribution to its grooming.

*392-393* ● Anything that moves attracts the attention of a cat, including the ears of its domestic companion.

*394* ● So different yet so similar: a month-old kitten is only slightly smaller than his Chihuahua friend.

*395* ● Crates, baskets, or boxes are irresistible attractions for cats and dogs used to living together.

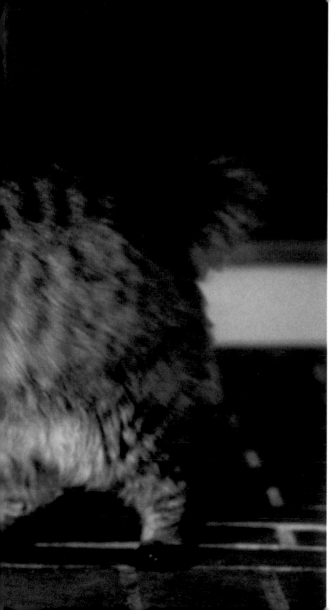

The dachshund is not a dog famous for its patience, but this one puts up wonderfully with a cat that is apparently "using" it to scratch its head.

A strange interview seems to take place between a cat and a sparrow (also domestic). The instinct to prey upon other animals, in kittens, is not clearly defined.

The rabbit seems rather indifferent to the red cat's show of interest. In any event, successful cohabitation is a matter of habit more than anything.

● A one-time encounter occurs between this tabby cat a couple months old and an extremely curious gray squirrel. Even the feline is interested, but, as seen just after, its dignity is slightly compromised by this show of excessive confidence.

404 ● A bullfrog becomes the target of a dangerous game for this adult cat.

405 ● The toad, an "alien" being, inevitably arouses the instinct to pounce and hunt in this spotted silver tabby.

*406* ● This bicolor British, like any good feline ever ready to hunt and flee, prefers elevated places. The saddle of a patient donkey is as good as any: besides being high up, it is mobile.

*407* ● Most of the time, relations between cats and other species are resolved basically by indifference. In general, the most interested is actually the cat.

● A beautiful tabby has no scruples about abandoning its predator personality
to its curiosity over a couple of sheep.

410 ● The temptation may be great, but experience teaches that hedgehog are dangerous.

411 ● With a tree frog, however, instinct gets the better of the cat, who starts to "play."

● Interest in sniffing
an almost equally
small Harlequin cat
is aroused in a piglet
a few hours old.

Caution comes first: with feline wariness a robust red tabby approaches a little bird family with two chicks.

Chickens and hens, and above all roosters like the one on the right, are anything but tame: the young cat on the left seems unaware of this, whereas the one on the right keep his distance for safety.

*From 418 to 421* •
Farm life is perfect
for cats: the young
felines find infinite
opportunities for action
and interesting subjects
to observe like
goats...or by whom
to be studied,
like this Persian.

# FIGHTS and SCUFFLES

● Acrobatic developments often accompany the games of kittens.

## INTRODUCTION Fights and Scuffles

Life is not always a bowl of cherries. In the wild it is rare because of abundant space and infrequent encounters; but in the city life of the modern cat, a scuffle may break out every now and then. The challenge is between rival males, and the most dramatic outcomes end in the winner inflicting a fatal bite on the neck of his adversary, but it almost never gets to that point. The world is full of old cats with chewed-up ears, the tokens of many battles. Winners or losers, they come out alive.

To see what happens when two cats meet, it is necessary to follow them on their secret excursions. Once the stronger cat has identified its opponent,

## INTRODUCTION Fights and Scuffles

IT APPROACHES AND HARANGUES THE OTHER CAT. TO SEEM BIGGER, IT WILL COMPLETELY DISTEND ITS PAWS AND RAISE THE LONG HAIR ON ITS BACK, WHILE ITS TAIL GIVES ITS BEST, LOOKING LIKE IT SPEWS FURY FROM ALL ITS PARTS. THE QUARRELSOME CAT ADVANCES SLOWLY WITH ITS EARS LOWERED, GRUMBLING, MURMURING, AND MEOW-ING STRONGER AND STRONGER. LIKE A RITUAL DANCE, AS IT PROCEEDS, IT RAISES ITS HEAD, TURNING IT FROM ONE SIDE TO THE OTHER, KEEPING ITS EYES FIXED ON ITS RIVAL. IT MIMES THE ATTACK, AS IF TO MAKE IT CLEAR WHAT ITS UNLUCKY VICTIM CAN EXPECT. WHAT SHOULD IT DO? IF IT IS A PEACE LOVER, IT WILL SHOW ITS INFERIORITY BY REMAIN-ING ALMOST CURLED UP, SUBJECTED AND SUBMISSIVE, READY TO RETREAT. IF, ON THE OTHER HAND, THE EN-

# Fights and Scuffles

## Introduction

COUNTER IS BETWEEN CATS OF EQUAL STRENGTH, THERE CAN BE LENGTHY MOMENTS OF IMMOBILITY, IN WHICH THE MUTUAL CHALLENGE IS COMPOSED OF SUCH IDENTICAL ATTITUDES AND STARES, LOOKING LIKE ONE CAT AND ITS REFLECTION. IT MAY ALL END IN NOTHING. OTHERWISE, SOMETHING SNAPS TO GIVE WAY TO A BATTLE, A FREE-FOR-ALL OF KICKS, BITES, SCRATCHES, MEOWS, AND FLYING TUFTS OF FUR. IN THE END, ONE OF THE TWO WILL HAVE TO GIVE UP AND STAY ON THE GROUND WITH ITS EARS COMPLETELY FLATTENED, BEGGING FOR MERCY. THIS IS THE CEREMONY, WHICH WAS LEARNED FROM KITTENHOOD. AS ADULTS, THEY HAVE ONLY TO DISTINGUISH BETWEEN PLAY FIGHTING AND SERIOUS FIGHTS, A FINE LINE AT THAT.

- Hair raised and back arched make this tabby seem bigger than it is.

*From 428 to 431* •
Mini-tigers in action
in the home.
The tactics of ambush
and intimidation
are basically the same
ones used by large
felines.

A friendly brawl comes to an end. After, the two contenders will go sleep in some removed spot.

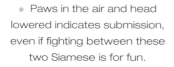 Paws in the air and head lowered indicates submission, even if fighting between these two Siamese is for fun.

This Korat-breed mother and son play at fighting. These cats, originally from Thailand, are playful and affectionate, but they rarely tolerate "intruder" dogs and cats.

438 ● A tortoiseshell cat prepares for the "final attack" against his play companion.

439 ● During a brawl, a little Siamese half-breed aims for his adversary's tail.

440-441 ● At first meeting, a Snowshoe, on the right, receives a rather unfriendly welcome from a tabby.

442 • Two kittens survey each other suspiciously, a normal phase in any encounter.

443 • Even a kitten like this silver tabby, given the necessary proportions, reveals its wild side in preparation for a wrestle.

# BEYOND the GARDEN

Perfectly camouflaged in the grass thanks to the stripes on its fur, a tabby explores the garden.

# Beyond the Garden
## Introduction

RY INSTINCTS START TO SHOW. PLAYING, WHICH SEEMS TO EXIST FOR ITS OWN SAKE, IS ACTUALLY A FORM OF STUDY. ANYTHING CAN BE AN ALLURING SOURCE OF EXPERIENCE: A MOVING OBJECT BRINGS ABOUT AN AMBUSH, A STATIONARY TOY INSPIRES A SURPRISE ATTACK, AND THE NEED TO CATCH THEIR OWN TAIL INCITES A WILD RUN. THE EXHILARATING SPECTACLE OF A KITTEN SETTING UP A TRAP FOR A BREEZE HE IMAGINES TO BE PREY OR WRIGGLING FURIOUSLY WHILE PLAYING WITH SOMETHING HE HAS ATTACKED EVOLVES INTO A FURTIVE STEP, COVERT OBSERVATION, IMPERCEPTIBLE TENSION IN THE TAIL, AND CONCENTRATED MOVEMENT OF ITS BACK LEGS AS IT BUILDS UP THE ENERGY NEEDED TO CONCLUDE A REGAL ATTACK.

- A mouse has ended up in the clutches of a cat, sparking off the famous "game" of the predator.

454 ● The pounce of a skilled consummate predator brings the cat to its prey.

455 ● Hard to catch, an expert hunter has caught a bird that had to be seized quickly.

456 • Envious of its environment, regardless of its size, cats explore
with all senses on alert.

457 • The excitement of exploration leads to risky jumps in spite of the lack
of swimming experience.

- Grass, as for their larger African cousins, is the greatest ally to hunting cats.

Nothing is more convenient than looking for prey at home: like any true opportunist, cats do not disdain an easy hunt in a bird house.

Cats, like this tabby and the Siamese on the right, adore elevated observation points, just like cheetahs or pumas. Positions of advantage, for smaller felines, are essential to survival.

● Cats – in this case a
blue-gray Chartreux –
are not lacking in
patience when hunting,
able to stay still for
hours while they lie in
wait for their prey.

466 • A cat positioned in the newly cut grass is an essay in "involuntary camouflage."

467 • Thanks to their wide field of vision, cats can observe their surroundings without moving their heads.

● The yard of the house, for a cat, is equivalent to the jungle for a tiger and the savannah for a lion. The need to control their territory is a crucial part of their nature.

A perfectly fixed stare indicates that the cat has chosen its prey. The approach begins.

The dazzling red
of a maple's autumn
leaves offers
an excellent screen
against perception.

S BIG OR SMALL AS IT MAY SEEM, THIS IS THE WORLD: A TERRITORY TO PATROL AND TAKE ADVANTAGE OF DAY AND NIGHT FOR THE SURVIVAL OF ONE'S LINEAGE. THIS IS AS TRUE FOR THE GARDEN AS IT IS FOR THE SAVANNAH, FOR CATS AS IT IS FOR LIONS, BECAUSE BEING PREDATORS HAS NOTHING TO DO WITH SIZE. "

474 ● A cat is ready to pounce, its paws gathered to its chest.

475 ● Crouched in position, a kitten flattens itself to the ground as much as possible.

● Great balance artists, cats dispose of their "higher senses" to survey the territory.

*478 and 479* ● The radiant, severe, somewhat "African" light helps to give these furtive half-breeds the look of fearsome predators, which Nature has actually made them.

*481-481* ● A few seconds and the hunt will come to a close, though the outcome is never certain.

482 ● That which flies low and is not too large must absolutely be grabbed.

483 ● Life in the fields involves running, besides long stake outs and grueling hunts.

● The game of cat and mouse is so impressive as to have become legendary.
Obviously, it is not about cruelty: for cats, hunting is an inalienable instinct
and a form of entertainment, which is carried out in this way.

● The hunt has been successful. The cat holds its prey firmly between its canines, shaped so as to leave no escape to a victim seeking to free itself.

*From 488 to 491* ● Keen and
patient observers, cats crouch as
they await the perfect moment to
seize the object of their desire, from
freshly drawn milk to flower vases
on which they have probably seen
a bug land.

492 ● A terracotta rooster is a strange animal, but it is still worth teasing to know what reaction it may have.

493 ● The cat is a little, proud predator, as its behavior often demonstrates.

• The colors of their coats noticeably helps young felines to carry out their needs to explore and investigate.

*From 496 to 499* ● Domestic cats love to drink "around" rather than in the container provided by their owner because they cannot stand the smell of the detergent with which the bowl was washed.

By day, cats trust their hearing more than sight, penalized by sunlight. Their moveable ears, on the other hand, can perceive the tiniest sound and locate its origin.

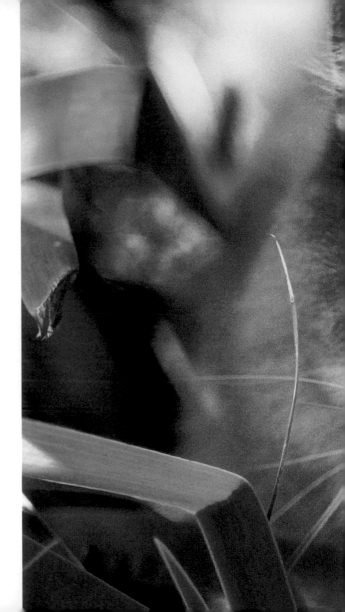

Cats patiently scan their world with all their "sensors" on alert. Their long whiskers, or vibrissae, provide them information on the distance of objects and the movements of their prey.

# Looking Pretty
Introduction

EVAPORATES, HAS THE SAME EFFECT AS SWEAT. AFTER HAVING BEEN IN THE SUN, THEY CLEAN FOR DIETARY REASONS, THEREBY INGESTING VITAMIN D, WHOSE PRODUCTION IS STIMULATED BY THE REACTION OF THEIR COATS TO THE SUN. WHOEVER HAS A CAT KNOWS THAT AFTER BEING HELD OR PET, IT USUALLY GOES OFF, SITS DOWN, AND BEGINS TO LICK ITSELF. CATS DO THIS BECAUSE OF THEIR ANCESTRAL INSTINCT TO ERASE THE FOREIGN SCENT AND REPLACE IT WITH THEIR OWN. THERE IS ALSO A PSYCHOLOGICAL NUANCE TO LICKING THEIR FUR. CATS DO IT WHEN THEY ARE UPSET, NERVOUS, OR EMBARRASSED. IT IS AN ALMOST UNCONSCIOUS AND UNCONTROLLABLE MOVEMENT, LIKE WHEN HUMANS SCRATCH THEIR HEADS.

- Cats, which learn the art of grooming from their mother, do not hesitate to use their teeth in tough spots.

It is clear how important cleanliness is for cats by the time they dedicate to it: about a third of their day.

A cat's rough tongue is endowed with hard quills that act like the tines of a comb during grooming.

514 ● To guarantee themselves precision in cleaning, cats make remarkable contortions.

515 ● Even during exploration of the outdoors, cats allow themselves  brief pauses for grooming.

Cleaning their fur is one of the first things kittens learn in order to be somewhat autonomous after a few days of life.

*518 and 519* ● An elastic and agile physique helps cats to perform their grooming sessions and allow them to reach every spot on their bodies.

*From 520 to 525* ● As "lazy" by nature and tired as it may be, a cat never forgoes cleaning before napping.

The occasional "scratch" is a additional activity in grooming, useful also for keeping muscles limber.

Sharpening their claws is indispensable to maintaining the proper length. Otherwise, the claw would not work correctly and would become a hindrance to the animal.

Cleaning sessions unfold in precise and always identical phases, starting from the front legs and ending with the tail.

• No dirt escapes the detailed attention of kitties, for whom grooming also plays an important relaxing role.

Licking their fur, cats also ingest vitamin D, beneficial above all when they are young. The two kitties are Birman mixes:
a black and white male and its sister, blue and cream.

Flecks of dust
or wool threads
have irritated this kitty,
which has interrupted
playing to clean
its eyes.

# ODE to LAZINESS

A litter has found a perfect place to take a nap, quiet and secluded.

# Ode to Laziness
## Introduction

MOVE THEIR EYES, WHILE THE REST OF THEIR BODY REMAINS COMPLETELY INERT.

THE PHASES OF SLEEP ALTERNATE: ONLY A THIRD OF THE TIME IS DEDICATED TO DEEP SLEEP, THE REST, LIGHT SLEEP. HOWEVER, TIME FOR DREAMS IS INDISPENSABLE, PROOF BEING THAT IF A CAT HAS LESS TIME TO SLEEP, THE DURATION OF DEEP SLEEP WILL INCREASE PROPORTIONATELY, AND THAT KITTENS, FOR THE FIRST MONTHS OF LIFE (THOSE WHICH WILL BE DECISIVE FOR THEIR FUTURE) ONLY KNOW THIS KIND OF SLEEP. DAYDREAMING IS ADULT STUFF: KITTENS ARE EITHER AWAKE OR IN THE LAND OF DREAMS.

• The yawn of cats is tied, as is ours, to the alternation of the phases of sleep/wakefulness.

Cats also choose a sleeping place on the basis of temperature, taking the best advantage of sunlight and body position to regulate heat.

Any place is good for sleeping, as long as it is safe...and it seems as if this kitten has made a bad choice.

With their eyes half open, cats are also aware while they sleep, ready to wake suddenly at the slightest sound and fall back asleep just as fast if all is quiet.

● Adorable lazybones, cats take advantage  of the features of the land and of the buildings to relax and, meanwhile, to observe the environment.

552 ● To sleep, for cats, may mean to dream of imprudent oneiric prey close at paw.

553 ● After a dozen minutes of vigilant sleep, cats are perfectly awake.

554 ● Between two steps of the house staircase, rest is more tranquil, and the group takes advantage of the situation.

555 ● A stretch after a nap helps to resume voluntary control of muscles.

556-557 ● The ears, ever erect, are ready to catch high-frequency sounds emitted by potential victims.

The daytime behavior of cats (right, a Maine Coon), in which brief phases of rest continually alternate with waking phases, reflects that of large wild cats, in some way saving energy for morning or evening hunting.

*From 560 to 563* ● Not only instinct determines the phases of sleep: apartment cats, sometimes, doze off more out of boredom than physical need.

● When they are calm, cats adore rolling around in the grass and on tracts of particularly odorous land. It is probably a habit related to their predatory nature, which encourages "masking" their own recognizable smell in order to go unnoticed.

Kittens sleep more and longer than adults during each phase of sleep, up to eight-tenths of the time is spent to "recharge."

Half-open eyes,
growing ever thinner,
head distractedly
reclined: sleep is about
to take the upper
hand…

In the wild, lengthy and continuous periods of sleep in kittens help to keep them safe and calm, so as to not attract other predators.

572 • Resting in a mass, these Norwegians kitties conserve heat: cats do not love cold, despite being very well adapted.

573 • A particularly wide yawn is accompanied by a lowering of the ears, as this pretty Persian silver tabby demonstrates.

*574-575* ● Naturally, the cleanest and softest places are favorites for sleeping…whatever their owner may think.

*575* ● There is no better pallet than a straw hat inside out, enveloping and safe.

576 ● Half awake, a little Ragdoll a couple months old allows a glimpse of the bright-blue tinted eyes of kittens.

577 ● Cats – in this case a young Maine Coon – tend to fall asleep suddenly, often maintaining the same position they had just a moment before dozing off.

● Despite seeming portraits of perfect feline bliss, sleeping cats experience sudden peaks of electrical brain activity, similar to those had when awake.

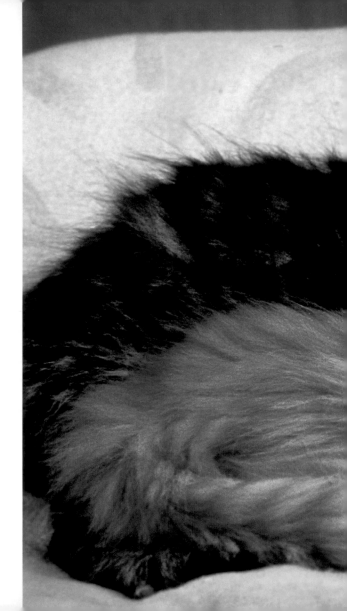

The owner's comforter is the most desirous place to rest, which does not seem to displease humans too much: sixty percent of cat-owners admit to letting them sleep on their beds.

- Explorations "beyond the yard" are tiring and therefore require some rest stops.

584 ● Cats invariably show their preference for warm, soft, and clean places.

585 ● The entire body becomes taut when stretching, from the tips of their claws, completely unsheathed, to the ears and the tip of the tail.

586-587 ● Inspired indolence for this "romantic"-looking cat.

# A WORLD of GAZES

- In the wild, the eyes of cats are probably the most well-known to and admired by man.

# A World of Gazes
## Introduction

ANIMALS ADAPTED TO DUSK, BECOMES A SLIT WITH ON-

LY TWO, SLIGHTLY OPEN, TINY PINHEADS AT THE ENDS:

THE FELINE GAZE TAKES ON A WILD AND A BIT ALIEN

LOOK LIKE THAT OF REPTILES AND REVEALS MUCH

ABOUT WHY THERE WERE TIMES IN WHICH CATS WERE

BURNED AT THE STAKE ALONG WITH WITCHES. HOWEV-

ER, THE SIZE OF THE EYE AND THE EXPRESSIVENESS OF

THE FACE ALMOST ALWAYS MANAGE TO SOFTEN THE

INTENSITY OF THIS IMPRESSION: ONLY THE CHARM RE-

MAINS OF THOSE MYSTERIOUS EYES, WELL SUITED TO

ILLUMINATING THE VISION OF THIS MOST ENIGMATIC OF

DOMESTIC ANIMALS.

*593 and 594-595* ● The limpid and luminous eyes of these two cats – a black European
cat and a tabby – are important indicators of their good health.

*From 596 to 599* ● Cats have excellent vision but are heavily penalized by intense light, which causes their irises to restrict and their field of vision to be reduced.

● The pupils in the irises of this Maine Coon are reduced to two vertical slits. The pupil reacts not only to light but also to emotions: in general, narrow pupils indicate trust, but also irritation.

*From 602 to 605* ●
Eyes in a frontal position
are indispensable
to predators, in as
much as they permit
them to precisely
calculate distances.

● Blue eyes sparkle in the gray coat of a Ragdoll, on the left, and a Sacred Cat of Burma. Intense and fascinating, the gaze of cats stirs admiration in humans. Young felines, however, do not like to be looked in the eye because, for them, it is a threat.

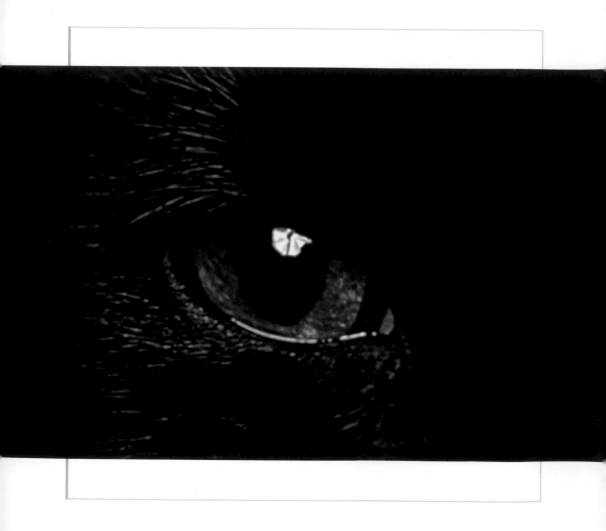

*From 612 to 617* ● A layer of highly reflective cells, the tapetum lucidum, give cats' eyes their extraordinary shine.

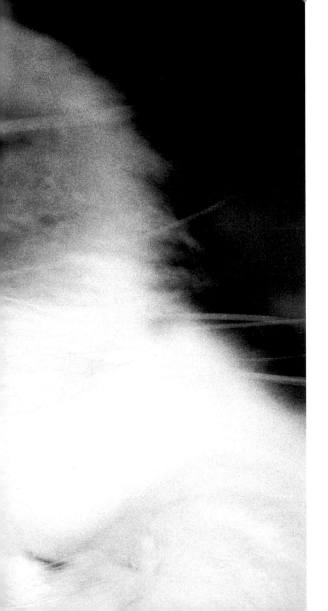

● Excellent peripheral vision allows cats
– which often seem "spellbound" while
watching nothing – to take in the greatest
amount of visual information possible
from their surroundings.

● The shade of the iris does not affect the vision of cats, which nonetheless perceive about a sixth of the colors visible to man, probably detecting only three colors.

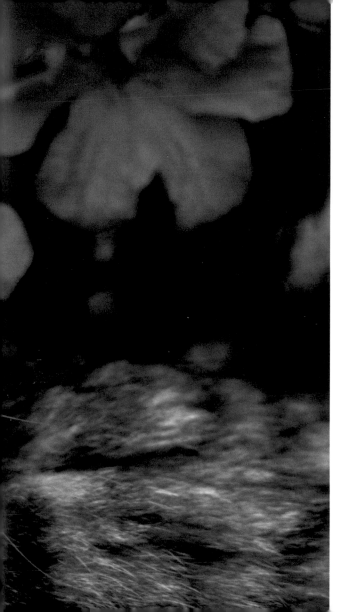

In bright light, the cornea is protected by an additional eyelid, the "nictitating membrane," which screens excessive light rays.

● Thanks to the intensity of their gaze, cats sometimes seem endowed with an expressiveness understandable to us, looking trustfully inquisitive or something like "accomplices," as in the case of winks.

*626 and 627* ● The eyes of two cats busy at "indoor" exploration feature dilated pupils, which allow them to observe a wider field of vision, denoting a certain degree of apprehension.

*628-629* ● Eyes and whiskers on alert, a cat senses tiny environmental variations, like rapid movements, which we are unable to perceive.

# CATS in the WORLD

With a proud stare, this kitten, which lives free on the Greek island of Santorini, seems boastful of the gorgeous panorama at its back.

# Cats in the World

Introduction

FORTUNATE ENOUGH TO PET THE SOFT FUR AND LISTEN TO THE GENTLE PURRING SOUND. PSYCHOLOGICAL WELL-BEING CAN BE ADDED TO THE PHYSICAL: A BOND COMPLETELY LACKING IN THE CONTRADICTIONS AND COMPLEXITIES THAT GOVERN THE LIFE OF MAN AND HIS PEERS CAN ONLY DO GOOD. CATS, THEREFORE, ARE EVERYWHERE. IN HOUSES, COURTYARDS, AND IN EVERY INHABITED PLACE, THEY EVOKE SOME IMAGE, FROM THE STREET RASCAL IN DUSTY MARKETS, TO THE QUIET AND SOLITUDE OF PLACES OF WORSHIP, TO THE ENJOYMENT OF SUMMER ON SUNNY ISLANDS. WHEREVER THERE IS A CAT, A DISCREET COMPANION, IT SEEMS TO BE PART OF THE LANDSCAPE.

● A Norwegian enjoys the chilly air of the Scandinavian winter from the windowsill.

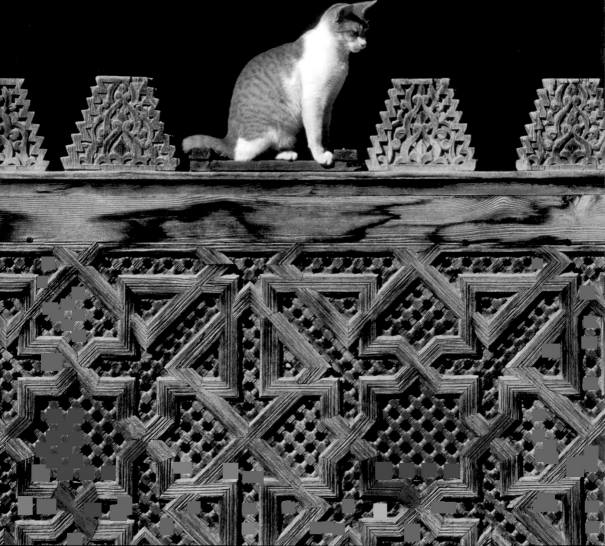

A meticulously carved wooden fence becomes the ideal position from which to observe the lively streets of Essaouira, in Morocco

637

A kitten begins its exploration of the streets of Tunis with caution.

The bright white of this cat's coat stands out among the skeins of wool drying in a dyeworks in Fez, Morocco.

A kitten has chosen the colorful courtyard of a Koranic school to nap: it can rest assured because Muslim custom forbids chasing it off.

● The triangular little windows in the wall of an Indian country home are perfect for satisfying a kitten's curiosity.

The funny pose assumed by this big cat while sleeping momentarily distracts from the gorgeous blend of colors in Alcazar de Siviglia, Spain.

The cats of Santorini live in complete freedom. It is common to encounter them strolling down the brightly-lit lanes or napping with nonchalance perched on walls high above the sea.

White and cobalt: the typical colors of the houses of Santorini blend into the Greek sky and sea, creating a background from which the acrobatics of an agile black cat stand out.

The smells, activity, and rhythms of the port are an irresistible call to cats living in a seaside town.

Any cat from the docks knows that patiently awaiting the return of the fishing boats may pay off in a tasty reward.

Thousands of cats live free in the streets of Rome. Far from resembling the emaciated felines that are often encountered in cities, Roman cats are often clean and well-fed.

*658-659* • Often, in mountain refuges like this one, in Switzerland, cats "work" with humans, both as companions and mouse catchers.

*660-661* • In a restaurant in Normandy, a striped cat basks in the sun, calm and indifferent. Furthermore, the plates are still empty...

In the eyes of cats, pumpkins carved for Halloween are but another curiosity to explore.

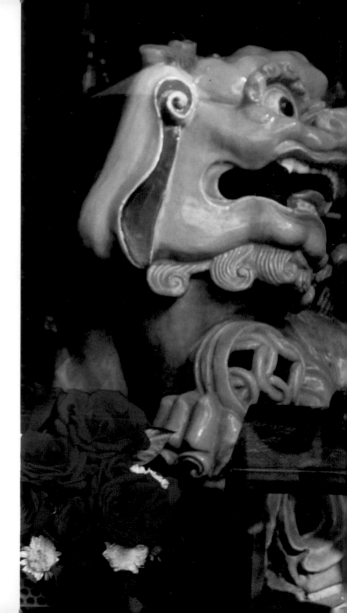

*From 664 to 667* •
As perfectly at ease
among ancient
Vietnamese ceramics
as among the shelves
of a Thai market: the
important thing is to find
a quiet and safe place
to nap.

- The calm and silent presence of a cat and her deeply sleeping kitten help this Tibetan craftsman to find the serenity necessary to finish a complicated carving.

Behind a meditating Buddhist monk sits a little cat, immobile and silent, almost a participant in the scholar's concentration.

In many parts of China, cats are still attributed divine powers, but these kittens have no need of this: their sweet and funny appearance is enough in order to be adored.

From the windowsill, the outside world can be observed in total safety and comfort, an ideal position from which cats can watch for hours.

A small movement or unusual sound is sufficient to stimulate the innate curiosity of two red cats, looking out the window to check on what is happening.

In line! To look out the little window, these five kittens deploy in strict military position.

A striped cat crouched on a ledge in Austria, on the left, and a kitten looking out a colorful window in India share the curiosity to survey the world from a windowsill.

# WILD COUSINS

Green eyes among the leaves: it is a wild cat *(Felis silvestris)* watching from the vegetation.

# Wild Cousins
## Introduction

CIAL SHEATHES UNDER THE SKIN WHILE WALKING, PADDING GINGERLY ALONG, OR RUNNING, MAKE THESE CATS' WAY OF MOVING SIMILAR TO ALL FELINES IN THE WORLD, WHEREAS THEIR ROBUST PAWS AND WARY ATTITUDE MAKE THEM RESEMBLE MORE PANTHERS THAN DOMESTIC CATS. THEIR WHISKERS, CALLED VIBRISSAE, INTERACT WITH THEIR ERECTILE HAIRS, GIVING EXEMPLARS OF THIS SPECIES EXTRAORDINARY SENSITIVITY, INDISPENSABLE TO HUNTING THE SMALL RODENTS ON WHICH THEY FEED. WITHOUT THEM, THEY COULD NOT BALANCE LIKE TIGHTROPE WALKERS ON THIN BRANCHES NOR MOVE SAFELY IN THE DARK: THEY WOULD NO LONGER BE THE WILD RELATIVES OF OUR HOUSECATS.

● A light, firm step, sensitive and vigilant eyes: the wild cat is a predator and it shows.

688 ● Truly frightening, this Scottish wild cat has assumed the absolutely most threatening stance in his repertoire of feline behaviors.

689 ● If it had remained immobile, this wild cat, perfectly blended into the mostly dark colors of his surroundings, would have been almost indistinguishable from the trunk.

Excellent hunters, wild cats dominate their environment and have no fear of climbing nor appearing out in the open, as long as, of course, they are in a protected reserve.

692 ● The wild cat, shown here with its thick winter coat, lives a solitary life.

693 ● Shy and crepuscular personality traits, found also in domestic cats,
are prevalent in nature.

694 ● Wild cats prefer the dense forest floor, whether of lowlands or mountains, where their superiority as predators allows them to live up to 15 years old.

695 ● The "game of cat and mouse" unites domestic and wild cats. The differences between them are actually only nuances, apart from the increased habitual nature in the former.

Mother cat, more alert than usual when she has kittens, has detected the presence of an intruder.

A pheasant is the trophy of this proud wild cat, whose victims are of course larger than those obtainable to a domestic cat.

*700-701* ● A wild cat uses the acute sense of smell with which it has been endowed.

*701* ● The forks of branches work as useful points of observation. The whiskers help the feline to keep its balance.

702 • The roundness of their head, dictated by the particular structure of their teeth, is very pronounced in wild cats, true "children of Nature."

703 • A wide yawn reveals the fearsome canines of wild cats, lethal weapons with which the animal generally snaps the spinal column of its victims.

*704* • Like their domestic cousins, even wild-cat kittens have bluish eyes.

*705* • A perfect medium-sized litter: three little ones, born in June-July, remain together while their mother hunts.

A true pouncing frenzy has overtaken this wild cat, which flings up an unfortunate rodent and then has fun catching it in mid-air.

The mother-kitten relationship often manifests great tenderness. Moreover, it is the only relationship of any particular duration for these solitary animals.

Though a wild cat may seem
a domestic species, the stubby tail, short
and marked with parallel rings of dark fur,
is unmistakable.

Often similar to a large tame kitty, wild cats change their appearance vastly when positioned in an elevated place looking down on an observer…or prey.

714 ● The sprint has begun: the designated victim must be quick in order to escape.

715 ● A noise has distracted this wild cat. In summer, the shorter and thinner hair reveals the fit and jumpy body of an agile predator.

*716 and 717* ● Three-and-a-half to four-and-a-half pounds heavy as an adult, this little black-footed cat *(Felis nigripes)* lives in the arid zones of southern Africa and must therefore obtain liquids through its prey.

*718-719* ● Proud hunter, this young and vigorous wild cat seems well aware of its own strength. Where there are no humans to threaten it, it has few natural enemies.

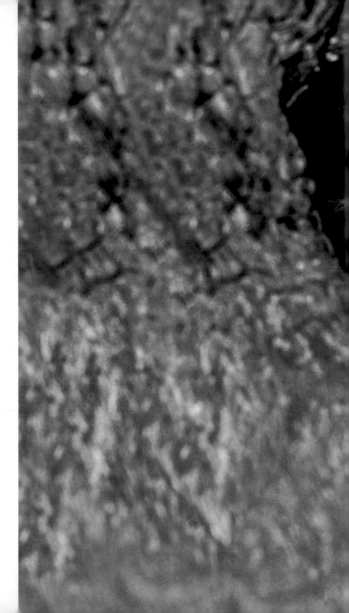

Wild cats, in general, use the abandoned lairs of other animals. A den is essential above all in early summer, when the little ones are born.

As charming in appearance as their "homebound" cousins, wild cats are, unlike the latter, untamable. Neither packs nor companions exist in their genetic memory.

When not busy patrolling or hunting, wild cats look like harmless tabby cats.

● Small but courageous, the sand cat (*Felis margarita*) lives in northern Africa and Asia, where poisonous snakes like the horned viper – which ends up decapitated – is one of its favorite "dishes."

# INDEX

## AUTHOR
Biography

### CATERINA
### GROMIS
### DI TRANA

Born in 1962, she studied Biology at the University of Turin, where she received her degree writing a thesis on Zoology. She then began to work with important museums such as the Regional Museum of Natural Science of Turin. Out of her work for various journalistic publications since 1997, among them the daily Italian newspaper La Stampa, several articles of an ethological nature have issued. Since December 2001, she has edited the column "From the World of Research" for the magazine of the Piedmont Region, Piemonte Parchi.

# PHOTO CREDITS

# PHOTO CREDITS

# PHOTO CREDITS

# PHOTO CREDITS

A kitten sniffs the scent of the daisies.